The Restless Sea

SAVAGE WATERS

CAROLE GARBUNY VOGEL

Franklin Watts

A Division of Scholastic Inc.
New York • Toronto • London • Auckland • Sydney
Mexico City • New Delhi • Hong Kong
Danbury, Connecticut

TO THE YOUNGEST COUSINS:
Danielle and Andrew Steg, Lauren, David, and Aaron Buzdygon

Acknowledgments

I am thankful to professor Peter Guth, Oceanography Department, U.S. Naval Academy, who took time from his busy schedule to read and critique the manuscript, and answer my many questions. His vast knowledge of the field and keen insight were reflected in his comments. I am also grateful to oceanographer Dr. Curtis Ebbesmeyer for providing information on drift cargo.

I am indebted to fellow writer Dr. Joyce A. Nettleton for her invaluable criticism, scientific expertise, and sense of humor. I am especially grateful to students Stephen, Daniel, and Joanna Guth for reading the manuscript from the kid perspective.

My sincere appreciation to my husband, Mark A. Vogel, for the encouragement and understanding that has become his hallmark. I would also like to acknowledge the many other people who helped either directly or indirectly.

Finally, my heartfelt thanks to my editor, Kate Nunn, for having faith in my writing ability and the talent to turn my manuscripts into spectacular books.

Photographs © 2003: Animals Animals/Earth Scenes: 65 bottom right (A. Paul Jenkin), 65 center right (Robert Lubeck); Corbis Images: 40 (Archivo Iconografico, S.A.), 12, 13 left (Tony Arruza), 68 (The Corcoran Gallery of Art), 34 (Rick Doyle), 71 (Stephen Frink), 54 (Darrell Gulin), 51 (Dan Guravich), 4 (Peter Johnson), 25 (Wolfgang Kaehler), 39 (David Lawrence), 50 (Danny Lehman), 65 top right (Christopher J. Morris), 43 (Guy Motil), 53, 69 (NASA), 64, 65 left (Dale O'Dell), 48 (Rick Price), cover, 28 (David Pu'u), 36, 37 (Carl & Ann Purcell), 47 (Jose Fuste Raga), 16 inset, 20 (Roger Ressmeyer), 16 (Roger Ressmeyer/NASA), 7 (Reuters/NewMedia Inc.), 60 (Galen Rowell), 19 (Joel Sartore), 10 (Michael T. Sedam), 23 (Kevin Shafer), 38 right (Richard Hamilton Smith), 1, 35 (Paul A. Souders), 45 (Stocktrek), 66 (Roger Tidman), 13 top right (Patrick Ward), 38 left (Ron Watts), 31 (Randy Wells), 24 (Ralph White), 65 top center (Michael S. Yamashita), 15 (Jim Zuckerman); Monterey Bay Aquarium Research Institute/Randy Wilder: 11; Richard Warner: 13 bottom right.

Illustrations by © Al Lorenz
Book Design by Marie O'Neill

Library of Congress Cataloging-in-Publication Data

Vogel, Carole Garbuny.
  Savage waters / Carole G. Vogel.
    p. cm. — (The restless sea)
Summary: Describes the origin of the oceans, oceanic waves, tides, and currents, and the volcanoes and earthquakes that can cause tsunamis. Includes bibliographical references and index.
  ISBN 0-531-12321-9 (lib. bdg.)   0-531-16682-1 (pbk.)
  1. Oceanography—Juvenile literature. [1. Oceanography.] I. Title.
  GC21.5.V635 2003
  551.46—dc21
                              2003005303

contents

CHAPTER 1
THE WATER PLANET 5

CHAPTER 2
THE ORIGIN OF EARTH AND ITS OCEANS 17

CHAPTER 3
WAVES 29

CHAPTER 4
TIDES AND SEA LEVEL 41

CHAPTER 5
CURRENTS 55

CHAPTER 6
THE GULF STREAM AND THE NORTH ATLANTIC GYRE 67

GLOSSARY 74

FURTHER READING 77

SELECTED BIBLIOGRAPHY 78

INDEX 79

THE WATER PLANET

In 1997 a colossal wave slammed into a cargo vessel in the North Atlantic Ocean, plunging 62 cargo containers into the sea. One container held nearly 5 million LEGO pieces, many of which were intended for kits depicting sea adventures. Although the spill occurred near England, the following summer LEGO pieces washed ashore along the coasts of Florida, Georgia, South Carolina, and North Carolina. Informed beachcombers were not the least bit surprised. How did they know the pieces were coming?

In January 1992 a cargo vessel ran into heavy seas far from shore in the North Pacific Ocean. Tremendous waves lashed the ship and swept a dozen cargo containers overboard. One container held 29,000 plastic bath toys, including yellow ducks, green frogs, red beavers, and blue turtles. Nine months later, thousands of the toys landed along the shore of southeastern Alaska. How did they get there?

Two years earlier, in 1990, a severe storm in the middle of the North Pacific battered another container ship. The rough seas hurled 21 containers holding nearly 80,000 Nike athletic shoes into the raging waters. Six months afterward, Nike shoes began to surface on the coasts of northern California, Oregon, Washington, and British Columbia.

Barnacles—tiny, hard-shelled animals—and oil covered the shoes, but a good scrubbing made the footwear usable again. However, the shoe pairs had not been tied together before shipping, so the shoes arrived on the beaches without their mates. Enterprising coastal residents set up swap meets to match up pairs. One of them, Steve McLeod, began to keep track of where and when some 1,600 shoes had landed.

Dr. Curtis Ebbesmeyer, an oceanographer from Seattle, read about McLeod and the drift shoes in the newspaper. He realized that the data McLeod had collected

This shipwreck is one of hundreds dotting the shores of the aptly named Skeleton Coast of Namibia, Africa.

could be used to study the path and speed of currents, gigantic "rivers" that flow in the ocean. For it was ocean currents that had swept the shoes from the spill site and brought them close to shore.

Ebbesmeyer contacted McLeod and other beachcombers. With the information they provided, Ebbesmeyer mapped the time and place of the shoe beachings. Then he shared this data with Jim Ingraham, a fellow oceanographer, who had created a computer model of Pacific Ocean currents. The model predicted the movement of currents. Using this technology, Ebbesmeyer and Ingraham were able to predict where and when more shoes and other drift cargo would land.

Each year fierce storm waves sweep some 10,000 containers into the sea. Among the items set adrift during the 1990s were:

- 34,300 hockey gloves
- a shipment containing tons of candy, including Tootsie Rolls, Hershey's Kisses, Riesen chocolates, and Werther's butterscotch candy (all in airtight packages that floated)
- 414 metal cylinders filled with arsenic—enough poison to kill half the population of the United States. (Fortunately, all of the arsenic was recovered before any harm could be done.)

Typically, only 2 percent of cargo set adrift in the mid-Pacific ever washes ashore.

Rhythms of the Sea

If you viewed Earth from space, the ocean would appear to be blue and still. But the tranquil scene would be merely an illusion. The ocean is in constant motion. Long before the space age, people who lived by the sea understood its basic rhythms—the tug of the tides and the rise and fall of waves. But other patterns seemed more elusive—the hidden landscape far beneath the surface, the relationship between ocean and climate, the complex paths of currents. Through the diligent research of thousands of scientists and chance events such as the tracking of drift cargo, the ocean has slowly revealed many of its secrets.

This digital image of Earth from space captures Hurricane Linda off the west coast of Mexico in 1997. This hurricane was one of the most powerful storms that ever formed in the eastern Pacific.

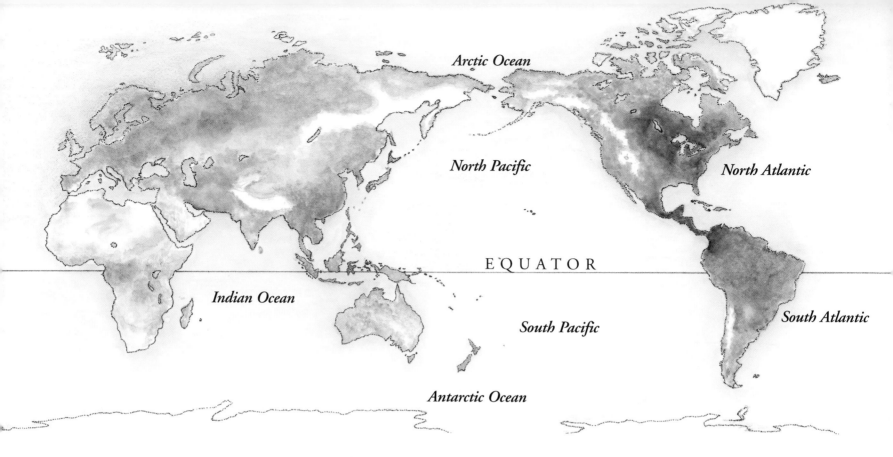

Arctic Ocean

North Pacific

North Atlantic

EQUATOR

Indian Ocean

South Pacific

South Atlantic

Antarctic Ocean

THE OCEANS OF THE WORLD

Although our planet is called Earth, it is in reality an ocean planet. The ocean covers nearly 71 percent of Earth's surface and holds 97 percent of the planet's water. Harbored far below its waves are canyons deeper than the Grand Canyon and mountains higher than the Himalayas.

Oceanographers—scientists who study the ocean—view the ocean as three different entities: the Atlantic, Pacific, and Indian Oceans. The largest of these, the Pacific Ocean, takes up more area than all the continents combined.

The oceans are all connected, and water circulates among them. The linked oceans are often referred to as the world ocean. Sometimes people mention two additional oceans—the Arctic and Antarctic. Oceanographers consider the Arctic Ocean to be the northernmost section of the Atlantic. And they regard the Antarctic Ocean as the southernmost part of the Atlantic, Pacific, and Indian Oceans.

Ocean Dimensions

Here is information on the surface area and depth of the oceans:

OCEAN	SURFACE AREA IN SQUARE MILES/SQUARE KILOMETERS	DEEPEST POINT	DEPTH IN FEET/METERS
Atlantic Ocean	41,081,040/106,400,000	Puerto Rico Trench	28,374/9,560
Pacific Ocean	69,115,400/179,700,000	Mariana Trench	36,198/11,034
Indian Ocean	28,350,500/74,900,000	Java Trench	25,344/7,725

Shallower, partially enclosed sections of the ocean are called seas. There are more than 50 seas, including the Mediterranean and the Caribbean, which are both part of the Atlantic Ocean. The term "sea" is also used as a synonym for ocean.

CONTINENTAL MARGINS

The oceans lie in a vast, deep basin rimmed by the continents. The oceans contain more water than the basin can hold, so they spill onto the continents. The oceans' edges are formed by the continental margin—the water-covered area of a continent that extends from the shoreline to the deep-ocean floor.

A continental margin consists of three zones: the continental shelf, continental slope, and continental rise. The continental shelf is a gently sloping area that

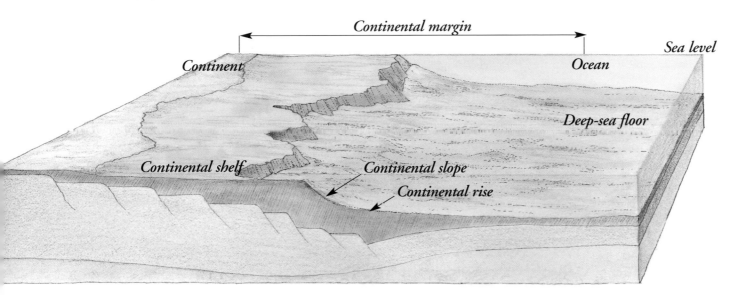

Continental margin

Sea level

Continent

Ocean

Deep-sea floor

Continental shelf

Continental slope

Continental rise

The Hawaiian Islands are the tops of large, gently sloping volcanoes that rise up from the Pacific Ocean floor. Shown here is the northeast coast of Molokai, the fifth largest of the islands.

begins at the shoreline and juts out an average of 40 miles (65 kilometers). Lying under relatively shallow water, continental shelves support much ocean life.

Dropping abruptly off the end of the shelf is the continental slope. The slope plunges steeply down to the deep-ocean bottom. Extending from the base of the slope is the gently angled continental rise. The rise is made of sediments—rock, sand, clay, mud, and debris from living things. Most of the sediments started out on land as solid rock that was gradually broken down by wind, rain, and ice. The agents of erosion—gravity, running water, moving ice, wind, and waves—swept the pieces of rock downhill. Eventually they reached the ocean, where they continued their descent, moving downward along the continental margin.

Wide continental margins, such as those ringing the Atlantic Ocean, experience little earthquake or volcanic activity. Narrow continental margins, such as those found on the outskirts of the Pacific Ocean, tend to be earthquake prone and volcanically active. Narrow continental margins are also likely to contain submarine canyons—deep gorges cut into the continental slope.

Monterey Canyon

Off the coast of central California lies Monterey Canyon, one of the most spectacular submarine gorges in the world. Rivaling the Grand Canyon in size and shape, the Monterey Canyon dips more than 2 miles (3.2 kilometers) beneath the Pacific Ocean surface.

Clinging to the steep, rocky canyon walls are exotic sea creatures that subsist on bits of food drifting by. Cracks and gaps in the walls provide shelter for fish, crabs, and other creatures. The silt-covered canyon bottom furnishes living space for animals directly on the seafloor or burrowed in the muck. The midwater, the watery world far below the surface, supplies abundant space for sea creatures to move but no place to hide.

Squat lobsters live along the California coast. Although they resemble true lobsters they are relatives of hermit crabs.

Submarine canyons were probably carved by turbidity currents—underwater avalanches. Powered by gravity, a turbidity current occurs when an earthquake or other disturbance shakes loose mud and soggy sand from a continental shelf or slope. The mud and sand cascade down the continental slope, eroding the seabed and picking up more sediments along the way. When the turbidity current loses momentum it dumps its sediments on the continental rise or deep-ocean floor.

RISING SEAS

During the twentieth century, the sea level rose 8 to 10 inches (20 to 25 centimeters) worldwide. Most climate scientists expect it to rise an additional 3 to 35 inches (9 to 88 centimeters) by 2100, depending on how rapidly Earth's atmosphere warms. The same scientists predict that the average global temperature will increase 2.5 to 10.4°F (1.4 to 5.8°C). The additional heat will cause glaciers

HOLDING BACK THE SEA

Over the years people have found many ways to hold back the sea.

(left) This seawall in Palm Beach, Florida, protects the shore from pounding waves.

(top right) The Thames Flood Barrier keeps London, England, safe from flooding caused by storm surges—walls of water driven by storm winds.

(below right) This breakwater in Rockland, Maine, protects the harbor from pounding waves.

13

and ice caps to retreat, releasing enough water into the ocean to produce the significant rise in sea level. Much of the meltwater will come from Greenland's shrinking ice sheet.

The scientists blame this global warming on human activity, chiefly the burning of oil, coal, and gas. The combustion of these fossil fuels releases carbon dioxide into the air. Carbon dioxide traps heat in the atmosphere in the same way that car windows trap heat on a sunny day. This is known as the greenhouse effect.

Tens of millions of people live in low-lying areas likely to be flooded by the rising sea. Among the most threatened are the Dutch with their vast amounts of territory below sea level.

Reclaiming Land from the Sea

There is an old Dutch saying that God created heaven and earth, but the Dutch created the Netherlands. The Netherlands is a small European nation bordering the North Sea. For more than 2,000 years, the Dutch have struggled to capture land from the North Sea and from inland lakes and wetlands—an amazing feat.

To hold back the water they erected dikes and then used canals and pumps to drain the land. The reclaimed territory, known as polder, has become fertile farmland. Beginning in the 1300s the Dutch built windmills to pump out water from behind the dikes. Today, electric or diesel-powered pumps have replaced most of the windmills. The Netherlands is about twice the size of New Jersey. Nearly 30 percent of the country lies on land that once lay beneath the sea.

Pushing back the sea has taken a terrible toll in human lives. Abnormally high tides and colossal storm waves have occasionally burst through dikes and inundated the countryside. Killer floods with death tolls of more than 50,000 people have besieged the Netherlands at least seven times since the year 1099. The worst one happened in 1530 and claimed 400,000 lives.

This historic windmill was built alongside a canal in Kinderdjik, Netherlands.

The Delta Works, a monumental flood control and land reclamation project, protects the southwestern corner of the Netherlands. Built between 1954 and 1986, it consists of four major barrier dams and six secondary dams. Only time will tell if the Dutch have finally succeeded in keeping out the sea.

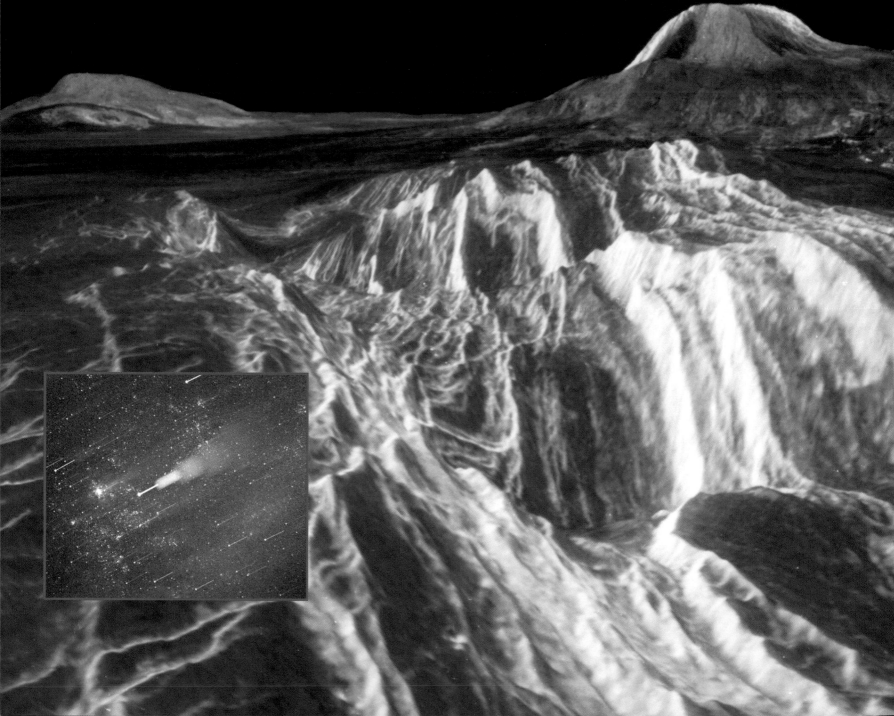

chapter 2

THE ORIGIN OF EARTH AND ITS OCEANS

If you could skyrocket back through time at the rate of one year per second, it would take you about 145 years to reach the period when Earth began. What did Earth look like when it was new? Nobody was alive back then to take snapshots of it. However, scientists have developed many theories about the origin of Earth and its oceans.

According to the most popular scientific theory, Earth's birth took place almost 4.6 billion years ago, and it was not a gentle one. It began with a super-nova—the explosive death of a massive star. When the star blew apart, a shock wave shot out in all directions.

A gigantic cloud of gas and dust drifted near the supernova. The shock wave overtook the cloud, squishing and heating it. The cloud started to spin and the material inside it began to clump together. The cloud flattened into a spinning disk. The hottest and the greatest amount of material collected in the center and became our Sun.

In the cooler regions of the disk, the remaining material crunched together into small particles. These particles slammed into each other, stuck together, and grew bigger with each collision. Some particles enlarged enough to have sufficient gravity to pull additional particles toward them. (Gravity is the "glue" that holds the universe together. This pulling power attracts objects to each other.) Over time the particles grew from specks of dust into pebbles, small rocks, house-sized boulders, and mountain-sized formations. From the largest objects, the planets began to take shape.

When Earth reached half its present size, there were perhaps 100 objects the size of the Moon or bigger in its vicinity. The violence increased as these rock titans crashed into Earth and into each other in a cosmic demolition derby. The catastrophic

The surface of the planet Venus as it appears today. Inset: The yellow cone of light is a supernova in the Large Magellanic Cloud galaxy that was photographed in 1987.

collisions blasted away any atmosphere and melted substantial parts of the growing planets.

Eventually the four inner planets—Mercury, Venus, Earth, and Mars—emerged. Rich in metals, each planet was a celestial blob of molten rock that gradually developed a hard crust. In the far reaches of the solar system, gases and icy objects formed the outer planets. Leftover material remained in the solar system as asteroids, comets, and other space debris.

The heavy bombardment of Earth ended nearly 3.8 billion years ago. But stray chunks of space debris still rain down on the planet every day. Most burn up as they zip through the atmosphere. The ones that survive the fiery passage and reach the ground are called meteorites.

THE BIRTH OF THE OCEANS

Strange as it may seem, during the first 800 million years of Earth's existence, the oceans did not exist. The planet's surface was a thick soup of molten rock. Any patches of crust that formed were ultrathin, brittle, and short lived. Heat produced by meteorite collisions melted the crust or erupting volcanoes punctured it.

Meanwhile in a process called outgassing, gases escaped from the molten rock and collected in Earth's developing atmosphere. The atmosphere was extremely hot and consisted mainly of nitrogen, carbon dioxide, and water vapor. Icy comets that bashed into the planet vaporized in the extreme heat and released more water vapor into the planet's gaseous envelope.

Earth's surface slowly cooled and hardened into a thin rocky crust. The atmosphere cooled too. Water vapor condensed into water droplets and formed an immense planet-cloaking cloud so thick that light could not penetrate it. Torrential rains pelted down from the cloud.

At first, rainwater falling on the scalding crust boiled instantly, flashing back into the atmosphere as steam. But the rain hastened the cooling of the crust, and eventually the water no longer sizzled away. Rainwater flooded the landscape and flowed into low areas. As hundreds of millions of years passed, the rain fell without interruption. A shallow, faintly salty ocean covered the entire surface of Earth. The atmosphere thinned and the cloud layer brightened, casting a dim light on the nascent ocean.

No continents existed yet. But some volcanoes grew into enormous mountains on the ocean floor. Poking through the waves, they became the first landmasses.

The Cradle of Life

Hydrothermal vents—hot springs on the seafloor—spewed out a hot, rich brew of chemicals. The chemicals provided the building blocks needed for life and the energy required to power it. The mystery of how life began remains unsolved. But some scientists believe that the undersea hot springs provided the habitat necessary for life to develop.

According to one theory, a community of one-celled organisms originated in hydrothermal vents about 3.8 billion years ago. These microorganisms became the

ancestors of all living things on Earth. No fossil evidence remains of these first life-forms.

The earliest-known fossils come from cyanobacteria, bacteria that appeared 3.5 billion years ago. Known also as blue-green algae, cyanobacteria still pepper the world's waters today. These microscopic organisms are a major ingredient of the scum that gives some ponds a blue-green tint. The ancient cyanobacteria shared their world with other bacteria and archaea—one-celled organisms that can thrive in extreme environments, such as hot springs or extremely salty water.

Before the first cyanobacteria came along, oxygen was tied up in molecules, such as water (H_2O) and carbon dioxide (CO_2). But cyanobacteria changed that. In a process known as photosynthesis, cyanobacteria captured the energy in sunlight. In this almost magical chemical reaction, the cyanobacteria used light energy to make their own food—a simple sugar called glucose ($C_6H_{12}O_6$)—from carbon dioxide and water.

During photosynthesis the cyanobacteria "passed gas"—they released free oxygen (O_2) into the environment. Over the course of 2 billion years, cyanobacteria expelled so much oxygen that the atmosphere gradually changed into an oxygen-rich environment. In fact, the bulk of the oxygen that you breathe today was originally liberated by cyanobacteria.

The buildup of oxygen in the atmosphere doomed many kinds of bacteria and archaea that had thrived in oxygen-free environments. About 1.8 billion years ago a new, larger single-celled organism appeared—the eukaryotes. They required oxygen to live.

The name *eukaryote* means "true nucleus." Unlike bacteria and archaea, eukaryotes have a distinct nucleus. Structures within a nucleus control all the cell's activities, including growth and reproduction. (In bacteria and archaea the material controlling cellular activity is strewn helter-skelter throughout the cell.)

From the first eukaryotes arose more complex living things—multicellular organisms. Some of these became the ancestors of all the plants on Earth. Others lacked the ability to manufacture their own food. So they developed a means of locomotion to move from place to place, and survived by devouring other living things. All the animals on Earth are descended from them.

Grand Prismatic Springs in Yellowstone National Park owes its brilliant colors to the heat-loving cyanobacteria and other microorganisms living in it. The temperature of the water ranges from 147 to 188°F (64 to 86°C).

21

Geologic Time Line

If we could pack the history of Earth into a single century, the birth of the solar system would occur on the first day of the century and humans would appear on the last.

YEAR (CENTURY SCALE*)	REAL TIME	EVENT
1	4.6 billion year ago	origin of Earth
8	4.2 billion years ago	oceans begin to form
13	4.0 billion years ago	Earth reaches its present size
17	3.8 billion years ago	bombardment by gigantic asteroids stops
17	3.8 billion years ago	first life appears
23	3.5 billion years ago	cyanobacteria evolve
45	2.5 billion years ago	oxygen builds up significantly in the atmosphere
60	1.8 billion years ago	eukaryotes appear
76	1.1 billion years ago	landmasses fuse together in a supercontinent called Rodinia
85	650 million years ago	wormlike animals and other soft-bodied animals appear
88	550 million years ago	Rodinia breaks up
88	540 million years ago	most of the major animal groups appear
88	510 million years ago	plants invade land
90	440 million years ago	the first fish appear
92	360 million years ago	the supercontinent Pangaea begins to assemble
95	225 million years ago	dinosaurs evolve
95	200 million years ago	Pangaea begins to break up
98	65 million years ago	dinosaurs die out; early mammals, insects, fish, birds, and flowering plants flourish
99	38 million years ago	first horses, elephants, and apes, and grasses appear
99.96	1.8 million years ago	earliest humanlike primates emerged
99.99	100,000 years ago	modern humans evolve
100	present	

*ONE YEAR ON THE CENTURY SCALE = 46 MILLION YEARS OF EARTH'S HISTORY.

The salt in these stacks was processed at a salt refinery alongside San Francisco Bay, California.

What's in Ocean Water?

Ocean water contains at least 80 different elements, including magnesium, sulfur, calcium, potassium, and carbon. Traces of gold and silver are found in it too, as well as dissolved gases and tattered pieces of dead bacteria.

The most abundant substance dissolved in ocean water is salt. It all water in the oceans evaporated there would be enough salt left behind to blanket all the continents in a layer 500 feet (150 meters) thick. That's about as high as a 40-story building or 10 humpback whales stacked end to end.

Anyone who has ever gulped a mouthful of seawater knows how awful it tastes. A swallow or two won't harm you. But because it's so salty, the more you drink the thirstier you get. Too much ocean water can make you sick.

The hot, mineral-rich water expelled by this hydrothermal vent on the ocean floor provides warmth and nutrients to chemical-eating bacteria. The bacteria, in turn, support other forms of life at the vent site.

Seawater is about 3.5 percent salt. Sodium chloride—table salt—makes up about 85 percent of the salt. The remaining 15 percent consists of calcium chloride, sodium sulfate, and other kinds of mineral salts. When salt dissolves in water it separates into particles called ions. Sodium chloride forms sodium ions and chloride ions. Calcium chloride splits into calcium ions and chloride ions.

Ocean salt comes from at least two main sources. One source is Earth's molten interior, which releases ions through volcanic eruptions. Another source is salt weathered and eroded from rocks on land. Rain or snowmelt washes the salt into streams and rivers. The waterways whisk the salt to the ocean.

Nearly 3 billion tons of salt pour into the ocean each year. Yet, seawater today is neither more nor less salty than it was 1.5 billion years ago. How is this possible?

Vast amounts of clay particles wash into the sea every year and absorb ions from the water. The clay particles settle to the seafloor, taking the ions with them. Marine organisms also remove ions, extracting them to form hard parts, such as shells. But this does not account for all the ions that leave the ocean each year. Scientists are still trying to puzzle out the processes. Hydrothermal vents may play a big role in the ocean's balancing act with salt. The vents remove some kinds of salt from seawater and add others. Although their role is not clear, some scientists believe that the entire ocean is recycled through hydrothermal vents every 10 million years.

The Dead Sea

Without massive recycling of salt the world ocean would become as salty as the Dead Sea, a large landlocked lake on the border between Israel and Jordan. Its salt content is 25 percent, making it the saltiest body of water on Earth. The Dead Sea lies at the lowest point on Earth's surface—about 1,300 feet (400 meters) below sea level. Water that flows into the Dead Sea has no escape route except for evaporation. As water evaporates it changes from a liquid to a gas and leaves its salt behind. (Salt does not evaporate.)

THE WATER CYCLE

Rain provides the ocean with much of its water. But the water doesn't remain in the ocean forever. The Sun warms water molecules at the ocean surface, supplying them with enough heat energy to evaporate. Most of the moisture in the atmosphere comes from the evaporation of ocean water. But water also evaporates from rivers and lakes, puddles and plants, even sweaty kids and panting dogs.

The water vapor rises in the atmosphere until it cools and condenses, turning back to liquid water in the form of droplets in a cloud. Eventually the droplets join and form larger drops. When they become too heavy to stay aloft, they fall back to Earth as rain. If the temperature of a cloud falls below freezing, the water vapor may form a solid—ice crystals. These crystals may fall as snowflakes.

Most of the precipitation falls directly into the ocean. But on land, the water flows into lakes and rivers or soaks into the ground. This liquid refreshment from the sky makes plant and animal life possible on land.

All the water on Earth is recycled through the water cycle, a continuous process that moves water through the environment. Water typically stays in the atmosphere for about 10 days before turning into rain, snow, sleet, or hail. On land it lingers as surface water for slightly more than two years or as

Precipitation over land

Groundwater

groundwater for nearly 400 years. Its sojourn into the ocean lasts even longer, about 3,900 years. But it can stay locked in ice at the poles or trapped deep in the ground for tens of thousands of years.

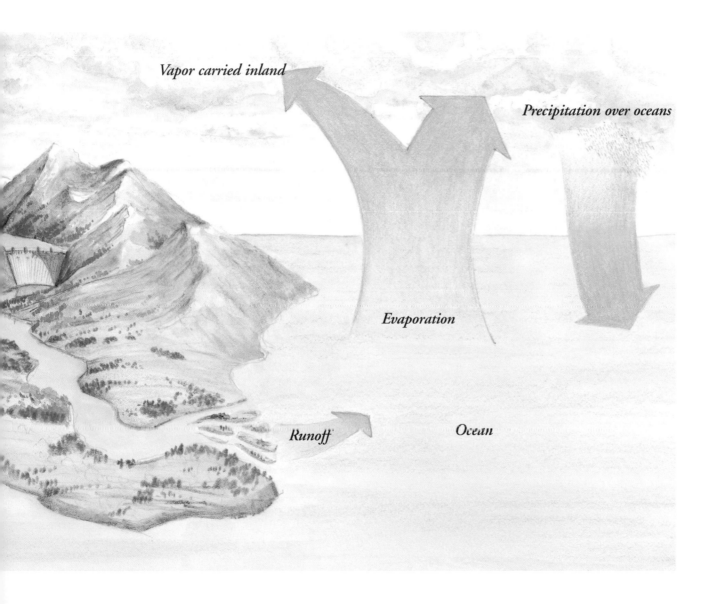

Vapor carried inland

Precipitation over oceans

Evaporation

Runoff

Ocean

chapter 3

WAVES

In 1942 the ocean liner *Queen Mary* was carrying nearly 15,000 American soldiers to Europe when a violent storm enraged the sea. A mountain of water—a rogue wave—slammed into the vessel, rolling it on its side and drenching the upper decks. There was no time to launch lifeboats. For several terrifying moments it appeared that the ship with all its passengers was doomed. Miraculously, the vessel righted itself.

Fifty-three years later, on September 11, 1995, the ocean liner *Queen Elizabeth II*, bound for New York, changed course in the North Atlantic to move out of a hurricane's path. Despite this maneuver the vessel encountered menacing seas with waves 60 feet (18 meters) high. At 4:00 A.M. a gargantuan wave shattered the windows of the Grand Lounge, 70 feet (22 meters) above the ocean surface.

Ten minutes later an even more ominous wave was spotted. Dead ahead loomed a wall of water 95 feet (29 meters) high. The captain later reported that it looked as though the ship was headed straight for the White Cliffs of Dover. The wave slammed into the vessel and was followed by two more giant waves. But the ship remained upright. The people aboard the luxury liner were lucky. Rogue waves can capsize ships or tear them in two.

Rogue waves arise when large waves come together to create titanic waves. Though rare and short lived, they can appear even in calm seas. In 1992 a 20-foot (6-meter) wave struck Daytona Beach, Florida, on a night when the typical wave was only 3 feet (1 meter) or less. Fortunately the beach was empty, so no lives were lost.

How Waves Form

An ocean wave looks like a rolling ridge of water. To understand how typical ocean waves form, all you need is a pan filled an inch (about 3 centimeters) from the top with water. Put your mouth close to the surface of the water and blow gently across it. Then blow harder. Small, even ripples should appear in the water when blowing gently. Hard blowing should produce bigger, choppier ones. Why?

Moving air—wind—traveling over water drags the water surface with it, creating waves. In the process, wind energy is transferred to the water. The faster the air moves, the larger the waves. Wave size also depends on the length of time the wind blows and the distance it travels over open water. High-speed, long-lasting winds that travel over great distances produce tall, steep waves. Although wind is the leading cause of waves, underwater earthquakes, landslides, and volcanic eruptions can create waves too, sometimes monstrous ones. They are known as tsunamis.

As a wave passes through water, the surface of the water rises and falls. The crest is the highest point of a wave; the trough, the lowest. The wave height is the distance between the crest and trough. The wavelength is the distance between one crest and another.

The time it takes for two crests to pass a specific point is called the period. Typically, waves along the Gulf coast have periods of about four seconds. Along the Pacific coast the periods average 10 seconds. This means millions of waves hit the shore every year.

Have you ever wondered why waves usually stop at the shoreline? In the open sea, waves appear to be moving forward. But actually, only the energy of the wave advances. The water stays in the same place. This is a good thing. Otherwise, ocean water would pile up on the continents and flood the land.

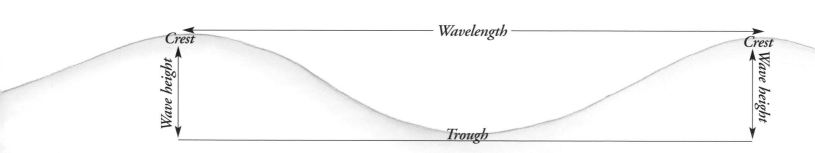

To observe what moves in a wave, tie one end of a rope to a doorknob and then pull the other end until the rope is straight. Jiggle the free end up and down to make a series of waves travel down the rope. You should notice that the rope moves up and down but does not go forward. (If the rope had moved forward, the free end would have been yanked out of your hand.) Only the energy traveled.

When a wave flows through the ocean surface, its energy makes the water particles move in a circle. They whirl forward and downward, and then around to their original position. You can't check this out for yourself, however. The particles are too small to be seen with the naked eye.

Below the surface, water particles orbit too. However, as the depth increases, the particles rotate in circles that gradually become smaller. At a depth equal to one-half the wavelength, the wave motion fades completely. If you were scuba diving at this depth or lower, you would be unaffected by the wave action above you, even if the waves were quite rough.

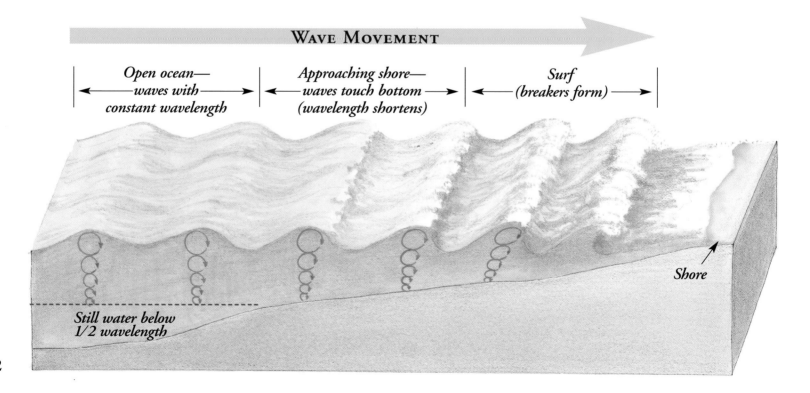

WAVE MOVEMENT

*Open ocean—
waves with
constant wavelength*

*Approaching shore—
waves touch bottom
(wavelength shortens)*

*Surf
(breakers form)*

Shore

*Still water below
1/2 wavelength*

Breakers

As waves approach the shore the water becomes shallower. The lower parts of the waves scrape the ocean bottom and slow down. However, the top parts of the waves continue to move ahead. The waves grow taller and the distance between them lessens. Soon the waves cannot support themselves. Their crests topple over onto the shore, forming breakers—foamy white surf. As the waves crash, their energy is released. The water rushes up onto the beach until the pull of gravity tugs it back into the ocean.

If you have ever waded along the shoreline you may have felt the pull of water rushing back into the sea. Known as undertow, the returning water sweeps sand, shells, and seaweed along with it.

Waves generated by powerful storm winds may travel thousands of miles. In deep water, the waves can lose their choppiness and spread out in a series of rolling mounds called swells. They continue to advance until they reach the shore or some other barrier that stops them.

At times, the waves from different storms cross paths. If two crests collide, the waves grow bigger. If a crest and trough intersect, the waves shrink in size. The vast Pacific Ocean spawns more storms than the smaller Atlantic and consequently more swells. In addition, the continental shelf off the Pacific coast of North America rises sharply and close to shore. It stops waves more abruptly than the broad, more gently sloping continental shelf off North America's Atlantic coast. As a result, waves along the Pacific coast are typically bigger and stronger than those on the Atlantic.

The Hawaiian Islands are the peaks of mighty volcanoes that soar high above the Pacific Ocean floor. Off the coasts of the islands lie coral reefs and underwater ridges created by lava flows. Some of these ridges and reefs redirect the energy of storm swells, creating monster waves and a surfer's paradise.

How Waves Sculpt the Shore

If you have ever been knocked down by a breaking wave, you know the power of the ocean. Where land meets the sea, waves are the chief agent of change. One

after another the waves keep coming. The shoreline—the boundary between land and sea—shifts with each rise and fall of the waves. Waves constantly shape the coast by building it up in some places and tearing it down in others. Along rocky shores, pounding waves act like battering rams. The force of their impact alone can fracture solid rock and knock fragments loose.

Waves carry large amounts of sand, rock fragments, and pieces of shells. These sediments came mainly from eroded shorelines or from rivers that have transported sediments from inland areas to the sea. Rolling in surf, the sediments can chip, scour, and grind down rocky landscapes, adding to the destructive power of waves.

Waves also break down rocks through chemical weathering. Seawater dissolves the minerals in some rocks, such as limestone, and hastens their disintegration. Gradually, the sea transforms boulders into smaller chunks of rock and then into stones and pebbles. These wave-scrubbed rock fragments eventually wear down into fine grains of sand. Relatively soft rocks, such as recent glacial deposits, erode rapidly, leaving bays and coves where cliffs once stood.

Sea Sculptures

Formations made from hard, compact rocks such as basalt or sandstone resist wave erosion longer and give rise to spectacular formations. Wave action can produce steep, jagged walls of rock called sea cliffs. Over time the scouring action of waves may hollow out a sea cave at the bottom of the cliff. If waves break through a sea cave's walls, a sea arch forms. Eventually, the top of the arch may collapse, leaving a spike of rock called a sea stack. Sea stacks also appear when softer rock in a sea cliff wears away leaving columns of more resistant rock. A terrace—a flat platform of resistant rock—may be all that remains of a towering sea cliff.

As waves slow they drop their sediments along the shoreline. Where sand and pebbles collect, they form beaches. Steep and narrow pebble beaches are common along rocky shores. Sandy beaches are found on gently sloping coastlines. Mudflats occur where rivers spill into the sea and dump their loads of sand and silt.

The color of beach sand provides a clue to its origin and composition. Along the Atlantic coast, light-colored sand covers the beaches. The sand consists mainly of quartz and other minerals found in granite, which was once part of the bedrock of the Appalachian Mountains. On the Hawaiian Islands, black sand formed from volcanic rock covers some beaches, while white sand, consisting of ground-up coral skeletons and shell fragments, blankets the rest.

Waves, currents, and wind constantly rearrange beaches. So why doesn't the sand disappear completely? On some beaches the wind direction shifts from day to day. In these places the sand removed one day is replaced the next. Where sand drifts mainly in one direction or washes out to sea, replacement sand comes mostly from river deposits.

Dams placed in rivers can rob beaches of replenishing sand. A dam traps huge quantities of sediments, preventing them from washing downstream. Along California shores, dams have reduced by half the amount of sand that reaches the coast.

Fairfax Island, with its beautiful beach, is part of Australia's Great Barrier Reef. The white sand comes from ground-up coral skeletons and bits of shells.

Sandbars, Spits, and Barrier Islands

Next time you visit the ocean observe how the water meets the shore. Waves usually strike shorelines at an angle, pushing sand, shells, and pebbles diagonally up the beach. The returning backwash from the waves pulls the loose sediments nearly straight toward the water. As a result of repeated wave action, the sediments move in a zigzag pattern along the coast.

The collision of the backwash with incoming waves produces a longshore current that flows parallel to the shoreline. These currents behave like rivers and can transport large amounts of sediments. If the shoreline curves, the longshore current slows and drops its sediments in the open water. A long underwater ridge of sand called a sandbar forms. If the sand bar rises above the surface and connects to the shoreline, it is called a spit. If the sandbar protrudes above the surface and doesn't link up with the mainland, it forms a barrier island. Some sandbars develop only during the stormy winter season when waves tend to be larger and sweep more sand away from beaches.

Ripples in sand

Sandbars channel the water flowing along the shore. If the water breaks through a sandbar, a dangerous rip current can form. A rip current is a narrow area where water rushes seaward. Rip currents pose a hazard to swimmers because the swiftly moving water can whisk them far from shore. To escape one, swimmers must swim parallel to the beach until they cross the current. Then they can head for shore.

Beautiful Whitehaven Beach on Australia's Whitsunday Island is the top of a sandbar.

39

chapter 4

TIDES AND SEA LEVEL

Jutting high above the ocean off the northwest coast of France is Mont-Saint-Michel, a fortified quasi-island with a magnificent medieval abbey. Perched atop a granite precipice, the fortress has endured ferocious storms, unimaginable waves, Viking attacks, and numerous wars. But Mont-Saint-Michel is not best known for its ability to survive adversity. It is famous for its tides.

At high tide, a stretch of water about a mile (2 kilometers) wide separates Mont-Saint-Michel from the mainland. But at low tide the water retreats, revealing a wide expanse of sand that links the island to the shore. The newly exposed land bridge, however, is not a safe place to stroll. The receding tide can leave pockets of dangerous quicksand. And at certain times, the returning high tide can roll across the sand faster than a horse can gallop. With a difference between low and high tides that may reach 45 feet (14 meters), an unwitting stroller could quickly drown if caught up in the onslaught.

Along most coasts the level of the ocean rises and falls twice a day. This sloshing of the sea is called the tide. It is similar to the back and forth sloshing of water that you can set in motion in a bathtub.

If you ever built a sand castle along the shore, you may have experienced the tide as the water crept slowly up the sand and swallowed your creation. Blame the castle's demise on the Sun and the Moon. The force behind the tides is the gravitational attraction between the Moon and Earth, and the Sun and Earth.

You may not have given much thought to gravity. But this amazing force exerts a strong grip on you and on all matter in the universe. It keeps the planets circling in their orbits and enables you to run, jump, and throw Frisbees. Without it, you could not take a single breath. It is gravity's invisible grasp that wraps the atmosphere around Earth.

Mont-Saint-Michel turns into an island at high tide.

41

THE MOON AND THE TIDES

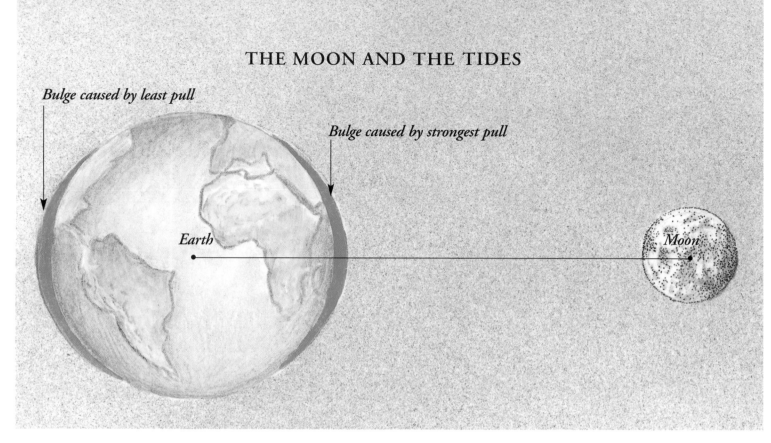

Bulge caused by least pull

Bulge caused by strongest pull

Earth

Moon

As the Earth rotates, the tidal bulges always line up with the moon.

Although the Moon orbits Earth at a distance of about 240,000 miles (386,000 kilometers), its gravitational pull wields great influence on the ocean. While wind action generates waves at the surface, tides tug on the entire sea from top to bottom.

The Moon's pull is strongest on the water on the side of Earth facing the Moon. The water lifts in a bulge, producing a high tide. At the same time the Moon's pull is weakest on the water on the opposite side of Earth. This water is left behind and creates another bulge and second high tide. Low tides occur halfway between the two high ones.

In the open ocean you cannot see the tidal bulge because it is less than 3 feet (1 meter) high and covers a wide area. But you can observe its impact along the coast. Where land meets sea, the average difference between low tide and high tide is 6 to 10 feet (2 to 3 meters).

As the Earth spins on its axis and the Moon orbits the Earth, the two tidal bulges also move. They remain aligned with the Moon. As the bulges travel, the locations they approach experience a rise in water level that gradually becomes a high tide. The process takes about 6 hours and 12 1/2 minutes. Then during the next 6 hours and 12 1/2 minutes the water level gradually drops and low tide occurs as the bulges move away.

Although the Sun is about 93,000,000 miles (150,000,000 kilometers) from Earth, it can make high tides higher and low tides lower. During a full Moon or a new Moon, the Sun and Moon line up with Earth. Together they create a more extreme effect on the oceans than the Moon produces alone. Spring tides result. Spring tides have nothing to do with the season. During a spring tide, high tides "spring" to their highest levels and low tides recede to their lowest.

Sometimes the Sun partially counteracts the moon's impact on the oceans. Small, or neap tides, occur during the first and last quarter of the Moon when the Sun pulls at a right angle to the Moon. Then the difference between high tide

SPRING TIDE

 *Earth*

 Moon

Sun

When the Sun, Moon, and Earth are in a straight line, during a full moon or a new moon, spring tides take place. High tides rise higher, and low tides fall lower.

NEAP TIDE

When the Sun pulls at a right angle to the Moon, neap tides occur. Neap tides cause the lowest high tides and the highest low tides.

 *Earth*

 Sun

 Moon

and low tide shrinks. The high tide is not as high and the low tide is not as low. Spring tides and neap tides each occur twice a month.

Oddly, not every place along a coast develops a daily rhythm of two high tides and two low tides. At the mercy of local conditions, tides are governed by the size and shape of the coastline and ocean floor. These factors determine the number of tides a day, the range between low and high tides, and how far and fast the tides travel.

The Bay of Fundy is a V-shaped bay in southeastern Canada. It separates the provinces of New Brunswick and Nova Scotia. The advancing tide enters the bay at its widest point and is funneled into an increasingly narrower and shallower area. At the narrow end, the tide becomes a tidal bore—a tumbling wall of water that sweeps up the rivers emptying into the bay. The bore varies from a mere ripple to nearly 6 feet (2 meters) high and moves so rapidly that the rivers appear to flow backward. Behind the bore the water keeps coming and coming, raising the level of the water in the bay.

Sea Level

Scientists measure the height or depth of features on Earth's surface using a standard called sea level. Mount Everest, the highest mountain on the planet, soars 29,035 feet (8,850 meters) above sea level. Mariana Trench, the lowest spot, plummets 36,198 feet (11,034 meters) below sea level.

Sea level changes with waves and tides, and it varies from place to place. So if the sea isn't level and it doesn't stay put, how can it be used as a reference point?

Local sea level is the height of the ocean at one instant of time at a particular location along a coast. If you measured the local sea level over a long period of time and then took the average, you would get the local mean sea level. Scientists take the average of local mean sea levels around the world to determine the global mean sea level—the average level of the entire world's ocean at a single moment. The global mean sea level is used as a reference in measuring the elevation of Earth's surface features. Since the 1970s, earth scientists have used altitude-measuring satellites to aid in determining the global mean sea level.

If you could smooth out the ocean surface by eliminating waves and tides, you would discover that the sea is not level. The unevenness is created by gravity. Without gravity, our planet could not hold the ocean in its basin. But, as you saw in the creation of tides, the pull of gravity is not equal everywhere.

Wherever the crust of the Earth piles up, such as in large mountains, the pull of gravity strengthens slightly. As a result, an underwater mountain pulls more water toward itself than a submerged flat plain. A small, smooth hill of water bulges above it. The mountains of the mid-ocean ridge, an underwater mountain chain, can raise the water at the surface by approximately 30 feet (10 meters).

Wherever the Earth's crust narrows, such as in deep underwater valleys, the pull of gravity weakens. Ocean trenches create gentle hollows in the water, where the surface drops 50 to 65 feet (15 to 20 meters). The slopes of these rises and dips are so broad and gradual that you would not notice if you passed over them in a ship.

Majestic Mitre Peak rises 5,551 feet (1,692 meters) above Milford Sound Fiord in New Zealand. The pull of gravity on this mountain is stronger than the pull on level ground at sea level.

46

ICE AGES AND SEA LEVEL CHANGES

Eighty percent of Earth's ice is locked up in a colossal ice sheet that shrouds Antarctica. This ice sheet, also known as a continental glacier, covers an area larger than Europe and the United States combined. It is about 1.6 miles (2.6 kilometers) thick. The remainder of Earth's ice lies in icebergs, alpine glaciers, and a vast ice sheet in Greenland. If all the planet's ice reserves melted, the sea level would rise about 200 to 230 feet (60 to 70 meters). Such drastic melting is unlikely.

Earth has endured many ice ages—periods when ice sheets and alpine glaciers covered much more territory than they do today. During these times, ice crowned up to a third of the land on the planet. The last ice age began about 75,000 years ago, when Earth's climates began to chill. (A climate describes the weather pattern that prevails over a particular region for a long period of time.) In the northern parts of North America, Europe, and Asia more snow fell each year than melted.

Decade after decade, snow piled up in layers. The immense weight of the snow squeezed the lower layers so tightly they changed into ice. The ice spread out in every direction. In North America an ice sheet up to 2 miles (3 kilometers) thick extended from the Arctic as far south as today's Ohio and Missouri River valleys. Alpine glaciers—thick rivers of slowly moving ice—appeared on high mountain-tops worldwide. At the peak of the ice age, 18,000 years ago, ice trapped so much of the world's water that the sea level had dropped 360 feet (110 meters) lower than it is today.

Glaciers chew up the land as they advance. Like a giant earthmover, a glacier pushes rocks and other loose material to its front and sides. At the same time, the glacier also plucks up rocks and other loose material from the ground beneath it. This rubble becomes trapped in the bottom of the ice. Together the moving ice and the embedded debris gouge and scrape the land.

During the last ice age, glaciers along the coasts of Canada, Norway, and Alaska bulldozed through existing river valleys on their way to the sea. The glaciers devoured the countryside, grinding gently sloped valleys into steep-walled valleys. When the glaciers reached the shore, they kept moving, scouring out long underwater furrows until the ice melted.

British scientists admire a large iceberg that is trapped for the winter by sea ice surrounding Antarctica.

This is one of the many glaciers that flow into College Fjord in Alaska. The dark streaks in the glacier are rock fragments that were broken off and transported by the ice.

About 12,000 to 10,000 years ago the climate warmed and the Ice Age ended. The glaciers began to thaw and the sea level gradually rose to today's level. Along the coast, the ocean flooded the steep-sided valleys, creating spectacular fiords.

The melting glaciers left behind piles of rocky rubble. Along its farthest line of advance the leftover jumble of debris was so great it formed immense ridges. Cape Cod, a peninsula protruding from the Massachusetts mainland, and the nearby islands of Nantucket, Martha's Vineyard, and Long Island formed from such ridges.

Scientists can't say for sure why Earth's climate swings back and forth between ice ages and periods of warmth. But they have some theories. According to the most widely accepted one, changes in Earth's rotation and orbit affect the amount of sunlight reaching the planet. A second theory links climate changes to fluctuations in the Sun's energy output. A third possible explanation is the movement of tectonic plates. Earth's hard outer shell is broken into about 30 immense slabs called tectonic plates, which support the continents and ocean floor. Over time, these plates gradually move, shifting the positions of landmasses and oceans. These changes impact global wind patterns and paths of ocean currents, which result in climatic changes.

The level of the ocean has been relatively stable since the last Ice Age. However, climate scientists expect a dramatic rise over the next millennium due to global warming. A rise of only 20 inches (50 centimeters) will threaten coastal cities, such as New York, New Orleans, London, Venice, and Shanghai. Other low-lying regions, including much of Bangladesh and the densely populated coasts of India, Egypt, and China, could be swamped.

Global warming is the greatest climatic change that Earth has experienced in the past 10,000 years and the greatest threat to the environment. With rising temperatures more water will evaporate from the oceans, resulting in increased moisture in the air and bigger storms when the moisture is wrung out. Temperature and rainfall patterns will shift. Worse floods, longer droughts, and more powerful hurricanes and blizzards will follow. Drastic fluctuations in climate will create havoc for

Global warming is causing the sea ice around Baffin Island in the Canadian Arctic to melt earlier in the spring and freeze later in fall. This is a disaster in the making for polar bears, which use the ice as a platform to stalk seals and other prey.

plants and animals that cannot adapt to rapid changes in their ecosystems.

Reducing the consumption of fossil fuels is the most effective way to combat global warming. A first step is energy conservation, reducing the amount of energy used in the home, school, workplace, and vehicles. A second is switching to alternative energy sources, such as nuclear energy, solar energy, wind energy, and even tidal power.

Tidal Power

Tidal power plants take advantage of the rise and fall of tides to produce electricity. They are practical only in bays, where a large difference between low and high tides occurs. At high tide, water rushes through the open dam gates. Then the gates close, trapping the water. At low tide, the water is released. It drops through tunnels that carry it past turbines on the way to the sea. The water spins the turbine blades, which turn an electric generator.

Deforestation—the cutting down of forests—has added to the carbon dioxide increase and the global warming threat. Trees sop up carbon dioxide during photosynthesis and use the carbon from it to make food. The carbon then becomes part of the structure of the trees. Some experts have suggested planting more forests as a way of removing carbon dioxide from the atmosphere.

What can you do to help? You can start by turning off lights when you leave a room, and shutting off the TV, radio, CD player, and computer when you finish with them. Walk, bike, or carpool with friends to cut down on car usage. Don't turn on an air conditioner if a fan will suffice. Plant a few trees and remember to recycle.

This view from the space shuttle shows the Strait of Gibraltar, a narrow channel of water separating the Mediterranean Sea from the Atlantic. The concentric waves moving into the Mediterranean are large ripples of water formed by tidal pulses from the Atlantic.

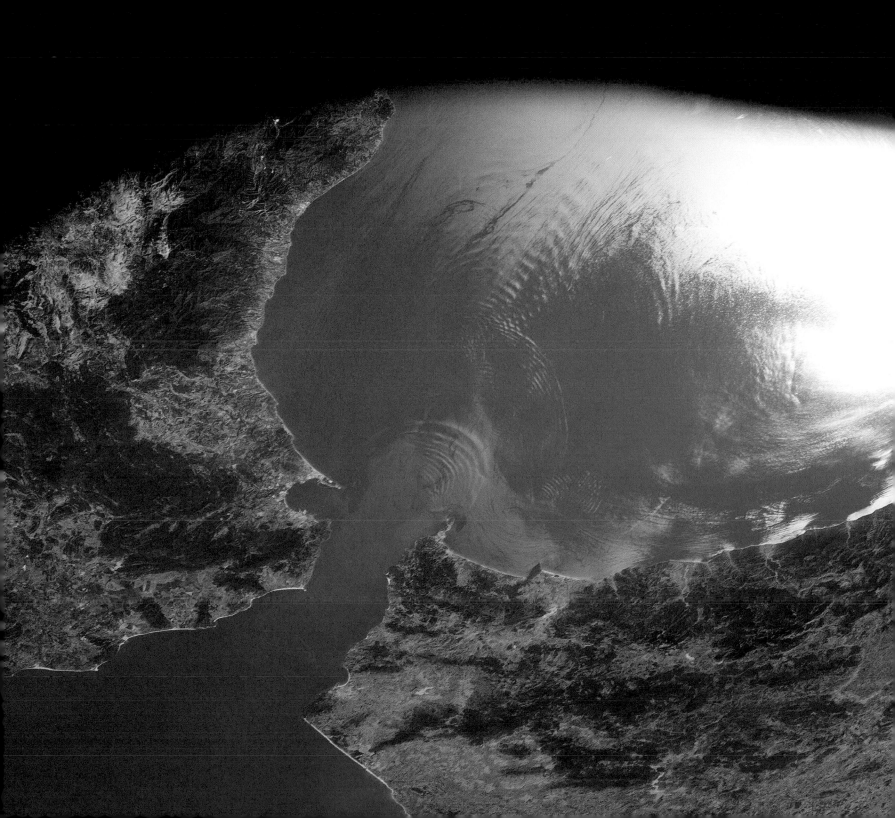

chapter 5

CURRENTS

Along the coast of northern California and southern Oregon giant redwood trees tower above the landscape. These trees grow nearly 370 feet (112 meters) high, making them the tallest trees on Earth. Redwoods are also among the oldest living plants: some live up to 2,000 years. Although they grow on land, redwoods depend on the Pacific Ocean for their survival during dry summers.

When warm, damp air offshore flows over cold water near shore, fog results. As the fog rolls in from the coast, it bathes the redwoods in moisture. Needle-like leaves on the trees act like collection nets. The water droplets in the fog collide with the leaves, where they join with other droplets to form larger drops. These large drops fall to the ground and sink into the soil. There, some of the water is absorbed by the tree roots. During a heavy fog so much water drips from a single redwood tree that a person standing beneath the branches is drenched.

The dramatic difference in temperature between the warm water offshore and cold water near shore is caused by the California Current. This current streams southward from Canadian waters, carrying cold water into the warmer waters along the west coast of the United States.

Like a gigantic river flowing through the ocean, currents transport water over huge distances. A current can be hot or cold, and it affects the climate of the land it moves past. Although a current resembles a river, it has no beginning and no end. Nor does it have a bank to contain it. Yet, a current follows a fairly predictable path. Some currents flow across the surface, while others skirt the ocean floor. Still others migrate from the surface to great depths or from great depths to the surface.

Wisps of fog flow through the majestic trees of Del Norte Coast State Park, California.

55

Oceans of Water and Air

Above the ocean lies another ocean, an invisible one without shores. It is filled mainly with nitrogen, some oxygen, and smaller amounts of water vapor, argon carbon dioxide, and other gases. You know this ocean as the atmosphere. It extends more than 600 miles (1,000 kilometers) high. Three-fourths of the atmosphere is squashed into a layer about 6 to 10 miles (10 to 18 kilometers) thick above Earth's surface. This lowest layer, the troposphere, is where we live and where rain, snow, and all other weather takes place.

The Ocean Conveyor Belt

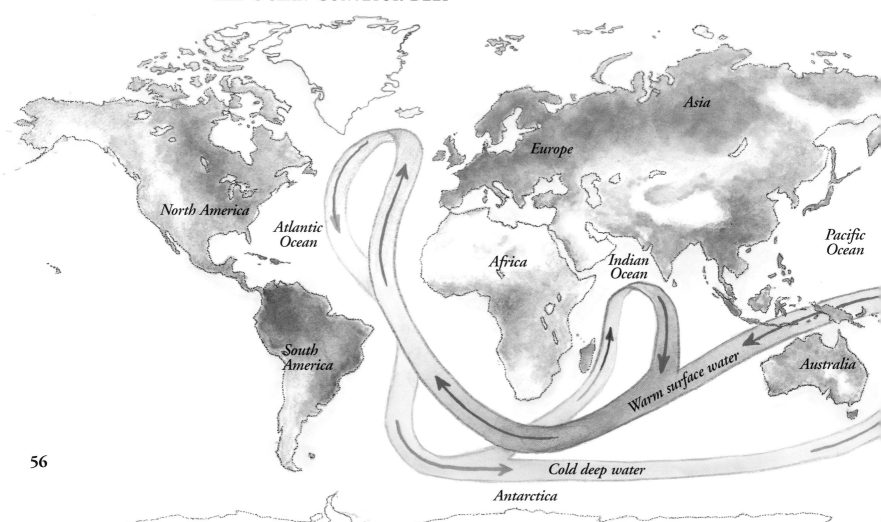

Like the ocean of water, the ocean of air moves constantly. Both are propelled by the Sun's energy and Earth's gravity, and their motions are intertwined. Sunlight strikes the Earth's surface, heating the land and sea. In turn, the land and sea radiate some of their heat, warming the air close above them. Day and night, warm air expands, and becomes lighter, rising bubblelike over the Sun-heated surface. Cooler, heavier air drops down to replace it. Winds—the atmosphere's version of currents—result. At the surface of the sea, air moving horizontally whips up waves and propels currents.

But the Sun does not heat the Earth evenly. Some parts of the Earth's surface receive more energy than others. The most sunlight reaches the Tropics, the area around the equator. The least reaches the Poles. As a result tropical waters are quite warm and polar waters are frigid.

Despite these extremes in temperature, the ocean is a gigantic reservoir for the Sun's heat. It stores the surplus heat of summer and releases it slowly during winter. In addition, it has an amazing capacity to move this heat over immense distances. As a result, the ocean regulates the planet's climates.

Currents shift massive amounts of warm and cold water around the world. Like an enormous conveyor belt, they transport warm water from the Tropics toward the Poles and move cold water back from the Poles to the Tropics.

Surface currents in the North Atlantic carry warm water from the Tropics northward to the polar region. In the polar region the water becomes frigid, sinks, and journeys south toward the equator. Near the equator some of the deep water warms and rises. At the surface, the warm water heads north again. However, the rest of the cold, deep water continues southward to Antarctica. From there it travels to the Indian and Pacific Oceans, where it warms, rises, and wends its way back to the North Atlantic. This round-trip, which may last a thousand years, helps to redistribute the planet's heat.

SURFACE CURRENTS

Just as wind creates surface waves, so it is the driving force of surface currents. Winds blowing continually across the ocean set surface currents in motion. But Earth's spin twists the path of currents. Known as the Coriolis effect, the rotation of the Earth causes currents to curve to the right in the Northern Hemisphere and to the left in the Southern Hemisphere. The Coriolis effect curves the path of winds, too. However, the paths of surface currents do not precisely match wind patterns. Hence, the paths of surface currents do not precisely match wind patterns. The sunken margins of continents and island clusters further bend currents, altering their course.

Trade winds—tropical winds that blow steadily from east to west—create some of the most powerful currents on Earth, the Equatorial Currents. These currents are broad bands of water that flow westward on either side of the equator. In time, the Coriolis effect and encounters with landmasses spin the South Equatorial Current to the south and the North Equatorial Current to the north, forcing both currents away from the Tropics.

Halfway to the Poles, the currents meet up with the prevailing westerlies, steady winds that stream from west to east. These winds, with some help from the Coriolis effect, rotate the currents to the east. The currents widen and move more slowly. Eventually the currents swing back toward the equator again, completing a nearly circular path called a gyre. Gyres are found in the North and South Pacific and in the North and South Atlantic.

DEEP-OCEAN CURRENTS

Differences in density within the ocean create deep-ocean currents. The density of seawater is affected by temperature and salinity. The colder and saltier seawater is, the higher its density and the lower it sinks.

The salt in seawater interferes with the formation of ice crystals. Like antifreeze, the salt lowers the temperature required for freezing. So seawater does not begin to freeze until the temperature falls to about 28.6°F (−1.9°C), and then it freezes from the surface downward.

Density

The oil and water in the containers are equal in volume. They take up the same amount of space. However, the water has more mass. It has a greater density. Density is the amount of mass in a given volume.

If two liquids have different densities, the less dense one will float on top of the other. Oil is less dense than water. Perhaps you have seen this in a bottle of unshaken salad dressing. The oil floats on vinegar, which is mostly water.

Seawater is denser than freshwater because seawater contains dissolved salt. Temperature affects density. If a liquid is cooled, the molecules move more slowly and become more closely spaced. Cold water contains more molecules and more mass than warm water of the same volume, so it has a greater density.

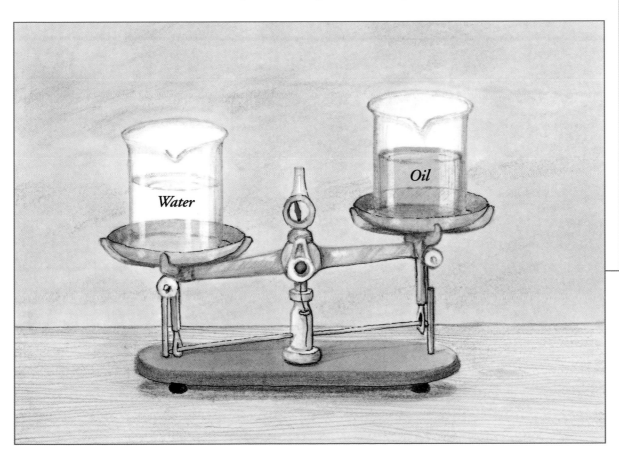

The *Yamal*, a nuclear-powered Russian icebreaker, clears a path through Calm Bay in the Arctic Ocean. The *Yamal* is equipped to cut through the thick ice of the polar ice cap to reach the North Pole.

As seawater turns to ice, it forms crystals of freshwater. The salt remains behind, increasing the saltiness and density of the surrounding water. The denser, saltier water sinks and can become part of a deep-ocean current hugging the seafloor. Less salty water streams in to replace it at the surface.

Deep-ocean currents flow sluggishly over the seafloor, lugging cold water from the Poles to the Tropics. Like surface currents, they are deflected by the Coriolis effect and the margins of continents. In the Tropics, the cold water mixes gradually with the warmer water above it.

The ocean is made of different layers, each with a distinct salt content, temperature, and density. Oceanographers can "read" these layers like individual pages of a book. Each layer varies only slightly from its neighboring ones, yet the layers usually remain separate. Seawater can travel horizontally for thousands of miles within a layer without mixing with the water above or below it.

The Heard Island Experiment

Scientists are using sound to find out if the ocean is heating up. At a depth of approximately 3,000 feet (1,000 meters), the salinity, temperature, and pressure create a layer that traps sound waves. The layer, dubbed the "sofar (sound fixing and ranging) channel" enables sound waves to travel more than 11,000 miles (18,000 kilometers).

In 1991 researchers set up an experiment near Heard Island in the southern Indian Ocean. Using underwater loudspeakers, they transmitted foghornlike sounds through the sofar channel to ships posted at listening sites around the world. The scientists determined precisely how long it took for the sound to travel from its source to each observation post.

Sound travels faster in warm water than cold water. Scientists reasoned that if the ocean were warming, a repeat of the experiment would show subtle changes in travel times. (A temperature rise of about 0.009°F [0.005°C] in the sofar channel will increase the speed of sound by a few seconds over long distances.) In 1994 results from a similar experiment in the Arctic Ocean suggest that the water had warmed slightly since the mid-1980s.

While sound experiments can measure temperature increases in the ocean, they cannot determine if the changes are caused by global warming or if they are part of a natural climatic cycle.

Some mixing of layers occurs in the polar regions when saltier, denser water at the surface descends to the seafloor to become part of a deep-ocean current. Mixing also takes place where there are upwellings. Upwellings are narrow, wind-powered, vertical currents. They appear along the western edges of continents where seasonal winds push surface water away from the coast. Chilly water from the lower layers wells up to replace the warm surface water.

Upwellings also occur along the equator. There, surface waters are pulled away from each other by the Coriolis effect acting on the southeast trade winds. Water from the deep rushes up to fill the void.

Upwellings play a crucial role in the ecology of the ocean. They bring dissolved nutrients from the depths to the surface. The nutrients come from dead organisms that plummet to the depths and decay. The nutrients fuel the growth of phytoplankton—microscopic plantlike organisms. Tiny animals graze on phytoplankton, and become, in turn, meals for fish, whales, and other marine creatures. Not only are sea creatures dependent on upwelling water, but the fishing industry is too. Upwellings create habitats that support one-third of the world's fish.

EL NIÑO AND LA NIÑA

Off the west coast of South America, near Peru and Ecuador, the nutrient-filled waters provide excellent fishing. Tiny fish called anchovies are particularly abundant there and have become a mainstay of the local fishing industry. However, every two to seven years in December, the trade winds that cause the upwellings change direction. The flow of cold water stops and warm water replaces it. The plankton die, and the anchovies either starve or swim to other places in search of food.

Hundreds of years ago, local residents dubbed this warming "El Niño," which is Spanish for "the boy." (The name El Niño refers to the Christ child, and was used because the current usually starts around Christmas.) El Niño is triggered by an unusual warming in the western Pacific, which creates an immense "pool" of heated water. The trade winds weaken and the heated water moves eastward toward South America, causing the temperature of coastal waters to increase as much as 15°F (8°C) above normal.

The impact of El Niño on plankton and anchovies is only a small part of its overall effect. El Niño is a planetary heat mover. It pushes heat out of the Tropics and dumps it elsewhere. In doing so it disrupts normal rainfall patterns, often with dire consequences. Typically dry regions may become drenched with rain. Areas accustomed to ample rainfall may get no rain at all. El Niño usually persists for 12 to 18 months, driving weather patterns wild across much of the world.

Some scientists speculate that El Niño may be growing stronger and recurring more frequently as a result of global warming. When El Niño retreats, it is sometimes followed by La Niña, "the girl," its opposite extreme. Since 1975, La Niñas have occurred half as frequently as El Niños, lasting 9 to 12 months. La Niña is a massive pool of abnormally cold water in the eastern Pacific. Like El Niño, La Niña turns weather topsy-turvy, but in a different way. La Niña takes expected weather patterns and makes them more intense. Wet regions become wetter; dry regions become drier.

Monsoons

More reliable than the winds that spur El Niño and La Niña are the monsoon winds that blow over North Africa, India, Southeast Asia, and the Indian Ocean. In summer, these winds carry warm, moisture-laden air northward from the Indian Ocean over the adjacent land. As the soggy air rises over the highlands of North Africa, India, and Southeast Asia, it cools and wrings out the moisture. Rains, among the heaviest known on Earth, soak the land below.

More than half the people in the world depend on these life-sustaining downpours. But there can be too much of a good thing. If the monsoons yield too much rain, massive flooding chokes the land, sometimes taking many thousands of lives. If summer monsoons fail to materialize, death and famine come to pass.

The summer monsoon creates a clockwise gyre in the Indian Ocean, which includes the rapid Somali Current along the eastern edge of Africa. Together, the monsoon winds and the Somali Current produce an upwelling that supports an extensive fishing ground.

In winter, the monsoon winds reverse and sweep cold, dry air from Central Asia over India and Southeast Asia. When the winds switch direction, so does the gyre. The Somali Current, now flowing in the opposite direction, slows. The upwelling and fish disappear.

The monsoons are caused by unequal heating. In summer, the land heats up faster than the water, so the air over the continent is warmer. As the warm air expands and rises, cooler air from over the ocean streams inland to take its place. In winter, the land cools more quickly than the ocean, causing the wind reversal.

WILD WEATHER

During La Niña, arid regions may become drier and wet regions, wetter.

(Left) Thunderstorms produced dazzling displays of lightning over parched landscapes but brought no rain. **(Right center)** Too much precipitation led to prolonged floods.

(Top Center) In 1997-1998, a drought caused by El Niño struck Indonesia, turning rainforests and banana plantations into dry fuel for rampaging forest fires.

(Top Right) The same El Niño was blamed for a mammoth ice storm, which downed electrical lines in Montreal and other parts of eastern Canada, as well as in northern New England, leaving thousands of homes without heat and electricity.

(Bottom) At sea, storms produced pounding waves that pummeled the shore.

chapter 6

THE GULF STREAM AND THE NORTH ATLANTIC GYRE

Off the east coast of North America runs the majestic Gulf Stream, a current so fast that it is sometimes called a maritime highway. The stream's deep blue color and clearness distinguish it from the dingy green of the surrounding water. Fish, turtles, seabirds, and whales flock to its plankton-rich edges in search of food. However, the clear blue waters of the stream itself are a biological desert, barren of sea life.

Benjamin Franklin, the great eighteenth-century American statesman and inventor, is often (but mistakenly) given credit for discovering the Gulf Stream. Before the American Revolution, Franklin served as the deputy postmaster of the American colonies. During that time, he was asked to solve a vexing problem: Why did British mail ships take two weeks longer to sail from England to the northern colonies than it took American merchant ships going in the same direction? What was so different about the route the British took that could account for their delay?

Franklin consulted his cousin, Timothy Folger, captain of a whale-hunting ship from Nantucket, Massachusetts. Folger told Franklin about the Gulf Stream and its strength: The current could be used to boost the speed of ships sailing from America to England. But it worked against ships traveling the other way. On days with weak winds, the current actually dragged ships back toward England. Nevertheless, the route the British took when sailing to America placed them squarely inside the stream.

American whale hunters had long known about the Gulf Stream because their prey could be found alongside the current but not within it. The whalemen had passed on their knowledge of the stream to American mariners, who heeded the advice to avoid the current when sailing home from England. The whalemen had also informed the captains of British mail ships of the current's force, but the

Humpback whales in the North Atlantic may find prey alongside the Gulf Stream but not within the waters of the Gulf Stream itself.

Ben Franklin (1706 – 1790) was the first person to publish a map of the Gulf Stream.

This image, as seen from the space shuttle, shows a loop of water that is ready to pinch off from the Gulf Stream.

British ignored them. According to Folger, the British "were too wise to be counselled [sic] by simple American fishermen."

At Franklin's request, Folger drew a chart of the Gulf Stream, and Franklin had it printed in England and distributed. However, the British sea captains chose to ignore the chart and Franklin failed in his attempt to improve mail delivery.

In 1513, long before Franklin was born, the Spanish conquistador Juan Ponce de León, chanced upon the Gulf Stream off the Florida coast. He was searching unsuccessfully for the fountain of youth. His navigator recognized the value of the Gulf Stream and word spread to other Spanish ships. Soon after, Spanish galleons laden with gold and other plundered New World treasure took advantage of the Gulf Stream to speed their way home.

Referring to the Gulf Stream as a stream, or a river in the sea, conceals its grandeur. The Gulf Stream is an astounding 30 to 45 miles (50 to 75 kilometers) wide, 1 to 2 miles (2 to 3 kilometers) deep, and carries about the same amount of water as 1,000 Mississippi Rivers bundled together.

The Gulf Stream is part of the North Atlantic Gyre, a large system of currents in the North Atlantic. Its beginnings lie within the Equatorial Current, which sweeps warm tropical water from near the equator westward through the Caribbean Sea into the Gulf of Mexico. After circling the gulf, the current is called the Gulf Stream. It squeezes through a narrow strait between Florida and Cuba.

The narrow passage compresses the Gulf Stream, forcing the water to flow more swiftly. (You can mimic this effect by partially covering the nozzle of a garden hose with your thumb as water gushes through it.) The Gulf Stream moves so fast here that sailors stranded on a raft off the Florida coast would be transported about 100 miles (160 kilometers) north a day by simply hitching a ride on it.

The Gulf Stream scoots along the East Coast of the United States at the rate of about 80 miles (130 kilometers) a day. North of Cape Hatteras, North Carolina, it widens, slows, and wanders farther from shore. The Gulf Stream rolls

past New York and New England toward Canada but does not flow within a set course like a river within its banks. From day to day its path can shift as much as 9 miles (15 kilometers). As the Gulf Stream sashays through the ocean, it forms loops. If a loop pinches off, it continues as a separate whirling ring of water. Measuring 60 to 120 miles (100 to 200 kilometers) across, the rings drift westward and last from six months to about a year before fading.

Off the Grand Banks of Newfoundland, the Gulf Stream meets the cold water of the Labrador Current, giving rise to thick fogs and sometimes violent storms. The Labrador Current plunges beneath the Gulf Stream and steals some of the stream's heat energy. Cooler and slower than before, but warmer than the surrounding water, the Gulf Stream swerves toward Europe.

Scientists call this northerly extension of the Gulf Stream the North Atlantic Current. It splits in two, with one branch veering past Iceland, Great Britain, and Norway, warming their otherwise chilly climates. The other branch wheels southward and becomes the cold Canary Current, which meanders past North Africa. It completes the gyre by spilling into the North Equatorial Current.

The Sargasso Sea

Inside the North Atlantic Gyre lies the Sargasso Sea, a quiet stretch of ocean two-thirds the size of the contiguous United States. Named for the seaweed that floats on its surface, the Sargasso Sea is a region of light wind and little upwelling. The sluggish waters lack the large quantities of nutrients required to ultimately support large predators such as tuna, swordfish, and other commercially valued fish species. As a result, the Sargasso Sea has been dubbed "the floating desert." However, this desert does bloom. Its pastures of seaweed support tiny crabs, shrimp, snails, and other small marine animals.

Perhaps the Sargasso Sea is best known as the nursery for most kinds of American and European eels. Eels are fish that resemble snakes. After hatching from eggs laid among sargassum seaweed, they begin life as flat, translucent larvae. They drift for a year or more in the Gulf Stream, eating and growing, before making their homes in the rivers and coastal waters of North America and Europe. When the adults reach the age of five or older, they migrate thousands of miles back to the Sargasso Sea where they spawn and die.

Sargassum algae provide food and hiding places for small animals living in the Sargasso Sea.

The Gulf Stream and the Mini-Ice Age

Without the Gulf Stream, Greenland, Iceland, England, and northern Europe would have much colder climates. The stream heats the air that eventually blows over these lands. In northern Europe, the Gulf Stream raises the temperature 9 to 18°F (5 to 10°C) higher in the winter than similar latitudes elsewhere. For example, London, England, lies at a more northerly latitude than Minneapolis, Minnesota. While Minneapolis averages about 50 inches (125 centimeters) of snowfall a year, London rarely glimpses a snowflake. Without the Gulf Stream, England would experience the same chilly climate as northern Canada.

About 8,200 years ago the Gulf Stream abruptly stopped flowing to Europe, leading to a worldwide deep freeze. Ironically, global warming triggered this cold snap. After the last ice age ended 10,000 years ago, the ice sheet, which covered much of northeastern North America, began to melt. In the Hudson Bay region of Canada, the meltwater created two humongous lakes containing more water than the five Great Lakes hold today. A dam created by leftover ice trapped the meltwater in Hudson Bay.

Eventually the ice dam melted and collapsed. The pent-up water gushed into the North Atlantic, unleashing as much flow as 100 Mississippi Rivers combined. The lakes took perhaps a year to drain. So much cold freshwater flooded into the ocean that it shut down the Gulf Stream and its warming effect.

In Greenland and Europe, temperatures dipped 6 to 15°F (3 to 8°C). The cold spell lingered for 200 to 400 years, thrusting the world into a mini-ice age until the Gulf Stream resumed its normal course. Some oceanographers today warn that global warming may bring similar consequences.

Mapping the Future

For centuries, human beings have struggled to understand the changeable nature of the sea and its impact on waves, tides, currents, and weather. At present, oceanographers know more about the ocean floor than they do about currents and gyres. This is not surprising because mapping submerged mountains and valleys with fixed borders is easier than investigating water in constant motion.

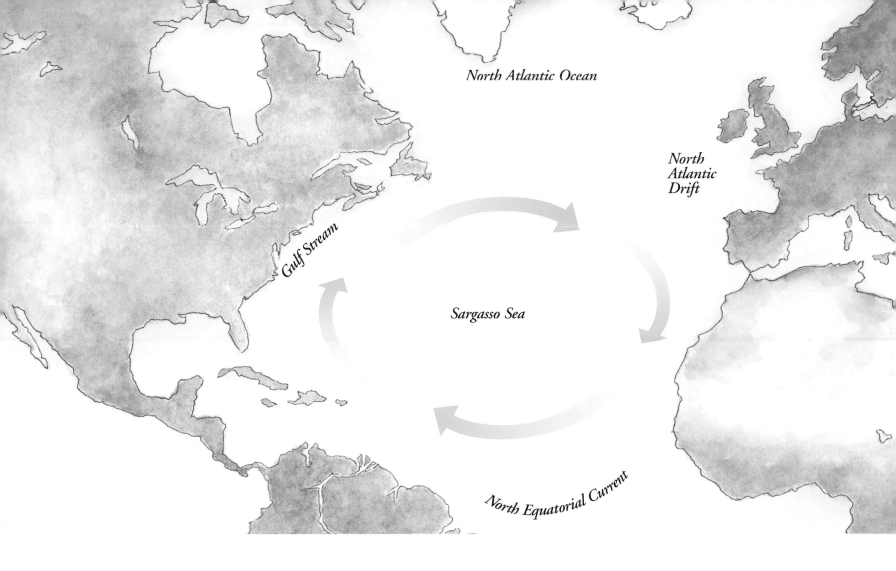

North Atlantic Ocean

North Atlantic Drift

Gulf Stream

Sargasso Sea

North Equatorial Current

Researchers are studying how solar energy, the Earth's spin, and the pull of the Sun and Moon work together to influence the motions of the sea. With the help of new technologies, they are mapping the paths of currents to better comprehend the ocean's influence on climate. This effort is paying off. In 1997 scientists were able for the first time to predict the onset of an El Niño.

Global warming remains a grave concern. Unless the nations of the world act quickly to reverse global warming, only time will tell if the dire warnings of a rapid rise in sea level or a return to a mini-ice age will come true.

glossary

ARCHAEA — one-celled organisms that can live in extreme environments, such as hot springs or extremely salty water

ATMOSPHERE — a mixture of gases that surrounds the Earth

BARRIER ISLAND — a ridge of sand that rises above the surface offshore but does not connect to land

BEACH — the accumulation of sediments along a shore

CELL — the basic unit of all living things

CLIMATE — the pattern of weather conditions for a particular region over a long period of time

COAST — the zone of land at the edge of the sea where waves are active. Also called the shore.

CONDENSATION — the process by which water vapor changes into liquid water

CONTINENT — a vast landmass surrounded by the ocean

CONTINENTAL MARGIN — the water-covered area of a continent that extends from the shoreline to the deep-ocean floor

CONTINENTAL RISE — a thick accumulation of sediments on the deep-ocean floor that slid down the continental slope

CONTINENTAL SHELF — shallow sea closest to the continent

CONTINENTAL SLOPE — steep incline dropping down from the continental shelf to the continental rise of the ocean floor

CORIOLIS EFFECT — the effect of Earth's rotation on the movement of winds and currents

CURRENT — a broad band of water that flows through the ocean

CYANOBACTERIA — oldest-known bacteria. Also known as blue-green algae.

DEEP-OCEAN CURRENTS — cold, density-driven currents that flow along the seafloor

DENSITY — a measure of the amount of mass contained in a volume of a substance

EL NIÑO — a massive pool of abnormally warm water in the eastern Pacific that has a worldwide impact on weather

EQUATOR — an imaginary line drawn around the center of the Earth halfway between the North and South Poles

Erosion—the destructive process in which water loosens and carries away rock fragments

Eukaryotes—cells with a distinct nucleus

Evaporation—the process by which a liquid changes to the gaseous state

Fiord—a steep-walled, submerged valley along a coastline carved by a glacier

Glacial deposits—rocks, sand, silt, and other debris left behind by melting glaciers

Glacier—a thick mass of ice that doesn't melt in summer. Propelled by gravity, glaciers flow slowly over the land.

Global warming—gradual increase in the average world temperature

Gravity—an invisible force that attracts objects to each other

Gulf Stream—a powerful, warm surface current that flows along the western edge of the North Atlantic Ocean

Gyre—the nearly circular path of water circulation in the open ocean

Hydrothermal vents—hot springs located on the ocean floor

Ice age—periods of time lasting tens of thousands of years when much of Europe and North America was covered by glaciers. The last ice age ended about 12,000 to 10,000 years ago.

Ion—an atom that has gained or lost an electron

La Niña—a massive pool of abnormally cool water in the eastern Pacific that has a world-wide impact on weather

Meteorites—space rocks that survive the passage through Earth's atmosphere

Mid-ocean ridge—undersea mountain chain

Monsoon—a wind that changes direction when the season changes

Neap tide—the time when the difference between high and low tide is at its smallest

Nucleus—the control center of a cell

Oceanographer—a scientist who studies the ocean

Outgassing—the escape of gases from molten rock

Photosynthesis—the process by which plants and plantlike organisms use light energy to make sugar and release oxygen

Phytoplankton—microscopic plantlike organisms that use the Sun's energy to manufacture food

Precipitation—water that falls from the atmosphere to the Earth's surface as rain, snow, sleet, or hail

Rip current—a strong, narrow current that rushes seaward from the beach

Rogue wave—a mountain of water

Salinity—the amount of dissolved salt in water

Salt—a compound that can be formed when an acid is mixed with a base

Sandbar—underwater ridge of sand

Sea—1. ocean. 2. partially enclosed, shallower section of the ocean, such as the Mediterranean Sea

Sea level—the height of the ocean

Sediments—small, solid particles that come from rocks or the remains of living things

Shore—the zone of land at edge of the sea where waves are active. Also called the coast.

Spit—a sandbar that rises above the surface and connects to shore

Spring tide—the time high tides rise to their highest levels and low tides recede to their lowest

Submarine canyon—deep gorge cut into the continental slope by turbidity currents

Surface currents—wind-driven currents in the ocean that move along the surface of the ocean

Swells—a series of smooth-topped waves that look like rolling mounds

Tidal bore—tide waters that converge at the mouth of a bay or river and move upstream in a wave that can range in height from a ripple to 16 feet (5 meters)

Tides—the daily rise and fall of the water in the ocean

Trench—a deep valley at the bottom of the seafloor

Turbidity current—an underwater avalanche

Undertow—the pull of water rushing back to the sea

Upwelling—a narrow, wind-powered, vertical ocean current

Water cycle—the movement of water through the environment

Wave—the movement of energy through water

Winds—large currents of air

World ocean—all the oceans of the world

further reading

BOOKS

Haslam, Andrew, and Barbara Taylor. *Make It Work!* Oceans. Chicago: World Book, 1997.

Heiligman, Deborah. *The Mysterious Ocean Highway: Benjamin Franklin and the Gulf Stream.* Austin, TX: Raintree Steck-Vaughn, 2000.

Lambert, David. *The Kingfisher Young People's Book of Oceans.* New York: Kingfisher, 1997.

Patent, Dorothy Hinshaw, with photographs by William Muñoz. *Shaping the Earth.* New York: Clarion Books, 2000.

WEB SITES

Dr. Curtis Ebbesmeyer is the scientist who tracked the path of the Nike sneakers, plastic bath toys, and LEGO pieces set adrift in the ocean. He maintains a Web site that provides updates on these spills and other interesting ones.
http://www.beachcombers.org/

NASA's For Kids Only Earth Science Program
http://kids.earth.nasa.gov/

NASA's Origins Program explores Earth's cosmic roots
http://eis.jpl.nasa.gov/origins/index.html

The Remarkable Ocean World: Benjamin Franklin and the Gulf Stream
http://www.oceansonline.com/ben_franklin.htm

What is El Niño?
http://www.pmel.noaa.gov/toga-tao/el-nino-story.html

What is La Niña?
http://www.pmel.noaa.gov/toga-tao/la-nina-story.html

The EPA's global warming site for kids
http://www.epa.gov/globalwarming/kids/index.html

selected bibliography

Duxbury, Alyn C., Alison B. Duxbury, and Keith A. Sverdrup. *An Introduction to the World's Oceans.* 6th ed. New York: McGraw Hill, 2000.

Kingsland, Rosemary. *Savage Seas.* New York: TV Books, 1999.

Prager, Ellen J. *Furious Earth.* New York: McGraw Hill, 2000.

Prager, Ellen J., with Sylvia A. Earle. *The Oceans.* New York: McGraw Hill, 2000.

Simons, Barbara Brooks, and Thomas R. Wellnitz. *Prentice Hall Science Explorer: Earth's Waters.* Upper Saddle River, NJ: Prentice Hall, 2000.

Tarbuck, Edward J., and Frederick K. Lutgens. *Earth Science.* 9th ed. Upper Saddle River, NJ: Prentice Hall, 2000.

Weiner, Jonathan. *Planet Earth.* New York: Bantam Books, 1986.

algae, 21, *71*
Antarctic Ocean, 8
Antarctica, 49, 57
archaea, 21, 74
Arctic Ocean, 8, *60*, 61
Atlantic Ocean, 8, 9, 11
atmosphere, 18, 26, 56–57, 74

Baffin Island (Canadian
    Arctic), *51*
barrier island, 38, 74
Bay of Fundy (Canada), 45
beach, 29, 36, *37*, 38, *39*, 74
breakers, 33

carbon dioxide, 14, 18, 21, 52,
    56
Caribbean Sea, 9, 68
cell, 21, 74
climate, 49–51, 55, 73, 74
cloud, 18, 26
coast, 5, 33, 74
condensation, 26, 74
continent, 8, 74
continental margin, 9–11, 74
continental rise, 9–11, 74
continental shelf, 9–11, 33, 74
continental slope, 9–11, 74
coral reefs, 33
Coriolis effect, 58, 60, 74
crest of wave, 30, *30*, 33
current, 6, 11, 36, 38, 39,
        55–65, 68, 70, 72, 74, 76.
        See also Gulf Stream;
        North Atlantic Gyre
    California Current, 55
    Canary Current, 70
    Equatorial Current, 68
    Labrador Current, 70
    Somali Current, 63
cyanobacteria, 21, 22, 74

dam, 14, 36
Dead Sea, 25
deep-ocean currents, 58, 61, 74
deforestation, 52
Delta Works, 14
density, 59–60, 61, 74
dikes, 14
drought, 51, 65

Earth
    cradle of life, 19–21, 22
    geologic time line, 22
    origin of, 17–18
earthquake, 11, 30
Ebbesmeyer, Curtis, 5–6
El Niño, 62–63, 65, 73, 74
equator, 57, 58, 74
erosion, 10, 24, 35, 75
eukaryotes, 21, 22, 75
evaporation, 26, 27, 75

fiord, *47*, 50, 75
fish species, 11, 22, 62, 70
floods, 14, 51, 65, *65*
fog, *54*, 55
Folger, Timothy, 67–68
forest fires, 65, *65*
Franklin, Benjamin, 67–68, *68*
freshwater, 59–60

glacial deposits, 35, 75
glacier, 49, *50*, 75
global mean sea level, 46
global warming, 11, 14, 51–52,
    72, 73, 75
glucose, 21
gravity, 11, 17, 33, 41, 46, 57,
    75
greenhouse effect, 14
Greenland, 14, 49, 72
Gulf of Mexico, 68

Gulf Stream, 67–70, 72, 75
gyre, 58, 63, 68, 70, 72, 75

Hawaiian Islands, 10, *10*, 33,
    36
Heard Island experiment, 61
high tide, 42–45, 52
hurricane, 6, 7, 29, 51
hydrothermal vents, 24, 25, 19,
    75

ice age, 49–50, 73, 75
ice crystals, 26, 58, 60
ice sheet, 49, 72
ice storm, 65, *65*
iceberg, 48, *48*
Indian Ocean, 8, 9, 63
Ingraham, Jim, 6
ion, 24–25, 75

La Niño, 63, 65, 75
low tide, 42–45, 52

Mariana Trench, 9, 46
McLeod, Steve, 5–6
meteorites, 18, 75
mid-ocean ridge, 46, 75
monsoon, 63, 75
Monterey Canyon, 11
Mont-Saint-Michel, *40*, 41
Moon, 42, *42*, *43*, 73
mudflats, 36

neap tide, 43, *44*, 45, 75
Netherlands, 14, *15*
North Atlantic Gyre, 68, 70
nucleus, 21, 75

ocean, 6, 8, 9, 10–11, 18,
    23–25, 33, 61, 62–63. See
    also sea

birth of, 18
    dimensions, 8–9
    elements in water, 23–25
ocean conveyor belt, *56*, 57
oceanographer, 6, 8, 61, 72, 75
outgassing, 18, 75
oxygen, 21, 22, 56

Pacific Ocean, 8, 9, 10–11, 33,
    55, 62–63
photosynthesis, 21, 75
phytoplankton, 62, 75
Poles, 57, 60
precipitation, 26–27, 65, 76

redwood trees, 55
rip current, 39, 76
rogue wave, 29, 76

salinity, 58, 61, 76
salt, 23, *23*, 24–25, 58, 59–60,
    61, 76
sandbar, 38, 76
Sargasso Sea, 70, *71*
sea, *12*, 13, *13*, 14, 23–25, 76.
    See also ocean
    elements in water, 23–25
    holding back, *12–13*, 14, *15*
    rhythms of, 6
    rising seas, 11–14
sea level, 11, 14, 46–52, 73, 76
sea sculptures, 35
sediments, 10, 11, 35, 38, 76
shore, 5, 30, *32*, 33, 76
shoreline, 9–10, 30, *33*, 35, 36,
    38
sound wave, 61
spit, 38, 76
spring tide, 43, *44*, 45, 76
storm surges, 13, *13*
storm waves, 14

Strait of Gibraltar, *53*
submarine canyon, 11, 76
Sun, 17, 26, 41, 43, *44*, 50, 57,
    73
supernova, *16*, 17
surf, 32, 33, *34*
surface currents, 57, 58, 76
swells, 33, 76

tectonic plates, 50–51
Thames Flood Barrier, *13*
thunderstorms, *64*, 65
tidal bore, 45, 76
tidal bulge, 42–43
tidal power plants, 52
tides, 6, 14, 41–45, 46, 52–53,
    72, 76
trench, 9, 46, 76
Tropics, 57, 60
troposphere, 56
trough of wave, 30, *30*
tsunamis, 30
turbidity currents, 11, 76

undertow, 33, 76
upwellings, 61–62, 76

volcanic eruption, 11, 24, 30

water cycle, 26–27, 76
wave, 6, 10, 29–39, 42, 46, *65*,
    65, 76
    how they form, 30
    movement of, *32*
    sculpting the shores, 33–35
windmills, 14, *15*
winds, 30, 36, 57, 58, 62, 76
world ocean, 8, 76

about the author

Award-winning author Carole Garbuny Vogel loves the ocean and lives 90 minutes from the beach. Her favorite water sport is boogie boarding, which is a lot like surfing but instead of standing up on the board, she lies flat. On beach days when the waves are small, Carole enjoys reading a good book or strolling on the sand looking for shells.

On workdays, Carole Vogel can usually be found "chained" to her computer, wrestling with words. She specializes in high-interest, nonfiction topics for young people. Among her many books are *Nature's Fury: Eyewitness Reports of Natural Disasters* (winner of the Boston Authors Club Book of the Year Award), *Legends of Landforms: Native American Lore and the Geology of the Land* (an NCSS/CBC Notable Social Studies Trade Book), and *Shock Waves Through Los Angeles: The Northridge Earthquake* (placed on the Children's Literature Choice List). Carole Vogel is the co-author of *The Great Yellowstone Fire*, which was named one of the 100 Best Children's Books of the Century by *The Boston Parents' Paper*.

Carole Vogel's books have been chosen for many reading lists, including Outstanding Science Trade Books by the NSTA-CBC, Best Children's Books of the Year by the Children's Book Committee at the Bank Street College of Education, and the Science Books & Films' Best Books for Junior High and High School.

A native Pennsylvanian, Carole Vogel grew up in Pittsburgh and graduated from Kenyon College in Gambier, Ohio, with a B.A. in biology. She received an M.A.T. in elementary education from the University of Pittsburgh and taught for five years before becoming a science editor and author. She keeps in touch with her readership by giving author presentations in schools and libraries.

Carole and her husband, Mark, live in Lexington, Massachusetts, where they enjoy frequent visits from their two children, who recently graduated from college. You can learn more about Carole Vogel at her Web site: *http://www.recognitionscience.com/cgv/*